The CISO Perspective

Understand the importance of the CISO in the cyber threat landscape

The CISO Perspective

Understand the importance of the CISO in the cyber threat landscape

BARRY KOUNS

&

JAKE KOUNS

it gp ™

IT Governance Publishing

IT Governance Publishing Ltd
Unit 3, Clive Court
Bartholomew's Walk
Cambridgeshire Business Park
Ely, Cambridgeshire
CB7 4EA
United Kingdom
www.itgovernancepublishing.co.uk

First published in the United Kingdom in 2011 by IT Governance Publishing.

ISBN 978-1-84928-182-9

This edition published in the United Kingdom in 2023 by IT Governance Publishing.

ISBN 978-1-78778-444-4

FOREWORD

Welcome to *The CISO Perspective – Understand the importance of the CISO in the cyber threat landscape*. In its first release, this book challenged security professionals to recognize that the serious and ever-changing nature of the security threats in 2011 demanded a strategic response and not just an operational reaction to the latest headlines. It posed the premise that it's time for chief information security officers (CISOs) to transition from being a security coordinator, to being an evangelist for risk management who also needs to be a technology innovator and a trusted adviser to senior management. More than a decade later, the security threats have only escalated and the challenge for CISOs to be more than just security coordinators has become a mandate for personal and organizational survival.

The goal of this book remains to challenge and guide information security professionals to think about information security and risk management from the enterprise level and not just from the IT perspective. The practical information will help CISOs understand how an enterprise view of information security, business continuity, compliance, safety, and physical security impacts risk and is crucial for the success of tomorrow's CISO.

PREFACE

This book is recommended for current and newly appointed CISOs, CIOs, and senior managers involved in, or interested in, information security management and technology risk management. Anyone thinking about a career in information security will benefit from the insights provided and the skills discussed. The topics are applicable to all industries and locations worldwide. All organizations will benefit from the material covered, but the guidance is most applicable to medium to large organizations with the complexity to warrant the CISO position. In addition, this book is a how-to guide for the information security practitioner to help them understand the goals of a CISO and an information security department. CEOs, CIOs, CFOs, and anyone else who has responsibility for managing a CISO can use this book to better understand the role and the best way to fully support the CISO function.

Frequent acronyms within this book include:

- CISO – Chief Information Security Officer
- CIO – Chief Information Officer
- CEO – Chief Executive Officer
- CFO – Chief Financial Officer
- CSO – Chief Security Officer

ABOUT THE AUTHORS

Barry Kouns is a security and risk management expert with more than 25 years of experience in information security consulting, risk assessment, and quality management. He formed and operates SQM Advisors, LLC, an information security, risk assessment, and IT service management firm that has led numerous organizations to ISO/IEC 27001:2013 certification. Kouns co-founded Risk Based Security, Inc., a vulnerability intelligence and data breach analytics organization, which was acquired by Flashpoint in 2022. He holds a BS in Statistics and an MS in Industrial Engineering Management. Kouns has earned the CISSP® designation and is a trained ISO/IEC 27001 Lead Auditor and ISMS Implementer, and is ITIL® Foundation certified.

Jake Kouns holds a Master of Business Administration with a concentration in information security from James Madison University. He holds a number of certifications including CISSP, CISM®, CISA®, and CGEIT®. He co-founded Risk Based Security, Inc., and is currently the Chief Innovation Officer at Flashpoint. He is well known from his presentations at security conferences including RSA, CISO Executive Summit, EntNet IEEE GLOBECOM, CanSecWest, and SyScan. He is also the co-founder of RVAsec, a Richmond, Virginia information security conference that has grown to host more than 500 attendees. Jake is the co-author of *Information Technology Risk Management in Enterprise Environments* and has also been interviewed numerous times as an expert in the security industry.

x

ACKNOWLEDGMENTS

The authors would like to express gratitude to our wives, Roxanne and Jill, for their wisdom and support during the writing of this book. A special thanks to Elora Nicole, Devin Jacob, Ashton Barry, and Savannah Rose for their contagious optimism.

We would also like to thank Robert Weiss for his help reviewing the manuscript during the production process.

CONTENTS

Contents

INTRODUCTION

This book is divided into eight chapters designed to introduce you to the CISO position. It discusses the tools used by the most effective CISOs and how current CISOs can grow with the challenges of the position. A brief description of each chapter follows:

Chapter 1: The nature of the CISO role

The CISO is bombarded with new issues on a daily basis, making it one of the most challenging positions in organizations today. CISOs find themselves responsible for the protection of the organization's information, but often reporting to the CIO who is rewarded for making the organization's information more readily available to all.

Chapter 2: The traditional CISO job description

The CISO is responsible for overseeing the overall corporate security strategy, security architecture, and security function. The scope of the role traditionally covers all implemented security technologies and services, including security applications, perimeter defenses, physical and logical access control, and access management for all employees, contractors, and visitors.

Chapter 3: The changing CISO role

The experience and skills that made yesterday's CISO successful no longer meet today's organizational needs. While being technology savvy is still very much a requirement of the role, today's CISO must have excellent communication and presentation skills, be able to understand everything within a risk management framework, and demonstrate keen business and financial acumen.

Chapter 4: The new CISO's toolbox

The time when a CISO could remain just a master technician is over, with no signs of it ever returning. If a CISO is to survive, they need to develop the skills of a leader, facilitator, communicator, and change agent. Today's CISO needs to prepare for and aspire to the role of trusted adviser to senior management, where they can translate information security threats into business risk and describe those risks in terms that stakeholders relate to.

Chapter 5: Risk management

The heart of any information security program is the information security management system (ISMS). And the foundation for any ISMS is the risk assessment and risk management methodology. The methodology used to identify, analyze, evaluate, and treat risk is foundational to any ISMS and sets the stage for identifying and appropriately protecting the organization's assets. An organizational-appropriate risk assessment foundation must be in place to ensure the protection of its assets and the CISO's success.

Chapter 6: The Information Security Management System

This chapter discusses the elements of a living, breathing Information Security Management System (ISMS) as defined in ISO/IEC 27001:2022, and the benefits of implementing an ISMS and obtaining third-party certification. Third-party certification of an organization's security program not only assures implementation of best-in-class security controls but can also provide the CISO with professional credibility and the organization with a competitive edge in today's cyber threat environment.

Chapter 7: CISO survival

In 2008, 29% of global organizations employed a CISO; in 2009, it was 44%[1]; and in 2021, 55%[2] reported having a CISO position. That's fewer than a 1% increase each year for the last 12 years. How many of the 2009 CISOs remain employed is not a figure easily found. How many of those CISOs currently employed will remain through 2023 will, for the most part, be determined by how well they prepare and position themselves for survival. This chapter discusses the techniques and strategies needed to better your chances of remaining in the CISO role.

---

[1] The Global State of Information Security Survey, 2010, conducted by PricewaterhouseCoopers.

[2] The State of Cybersecurity Leadership and Readiness Survey, 2021, conducted by Navisite.

Chapter 8: Summary – You become what you think about

With the daily challenges facing a CISO, a focus on the right things and proper consideration of your role in identifying, communicating, and mitigating risk are essential. Making a conscious effort to think about what you know you need to do and what you want to become can have a powerful impact on your job effectiveness and your success in life, if you think about the right things. This chapter offers guidance on how to properly align your thinking with the needs and security challenges of today's organizations.

CHAPTER 1: THE NATURE OF THE CISO ROLE

"Technology presumes there's just one right way to do things and there never is."

Robert M. Pirsig
American Writer and Philosopher

Chief Information Security Officers (CISOs) are bombarded with new challenges every day. In fact, they change so fast it makes little sense to list them here since they will be replaced with others tomorrow. Instead, let's take a look at the very nature of the role and why it may well be one of the most unique and challenging in organizations.

Information security and the CISO role have for far too long been about implementing the latest security technology. Yes, security technology plays a large role in businesses today, but identifying and implementing technology should be to address a specific organization risk, and even then it is only a small part of the information security challenge faced by CISOs. Indeed, in today's security-successful organization, implementing the right technology to address the organization's risks is a critical but small part of the CISO's leadership role.

As a CISO, you will quickly discover that you are in a dilemma of sorts: You are responsible for the protection of the organization's information, but often you find yourself reporting to the CIO who is rewarded for making the organization's information more readily available to all. CISOs are in the business of securely managing the flow of information, not just locking it down. Information that was once a static entity that stayed where you stored it within the perimeter is now on the move, constantly flowing in and out of the organization. With information traveling to home offices/remote worksites, crossing international boundaries via laptops, thumb drives, smartphones, and all means of Internet connectivity, perimeter-based security is a thing of the distant past.

The beginning

The title of CISO burst onto the national scene in the US soon after the terrorist attacks on September 11, 2001. Creating a dedicated office of the CISO became the go-to answer for many organizations anxious to demonstrate a serious commitment to information security, disaster recovery planning, and business continuity. A CISO was appointed/hired because company executives believed a dedicated office and an appointed executive would be viewed by clients and regulators as the best way to address the inconvenient security 'issue.'

Many of the first CISOs came from the ranks of current employees who were simply recast into the new role. Most CISO offices were set up with the belief that responsibility for the organization's information security is a task like any other that could be assigned to a single person in the company. With few to no staff and limited budget, minimal formal security education, and a reporting structure through the CFO, CIO, or lower, the first CISOs were simply tolerated and only appreciated during an audit or recovery from a crisis. You would be wise to avoid accepting any CISO role that has these characteristics.

Forever increasing threats

Law enforcement investigations consistently discover that cyber crime is an organized global business, often backed by governments, that hires, equips, and directs hackers in their attacks on financial institutions and personal accounts. The disclosure of 30,657 new software vulnerabilities in 2021 far exceeded the number reported in 2011: just 8,301. On average, the number of newly disclosed software vulnerabilities increased 14.6% year-over-year.[3] The number of reported data breaches in 2011 amounted to just 1,309 compared to 5,210 reported in 2021. While off the high mark of 7,674 set in 2019, the 2021 number is most likely impacted by the slow reporting caused by the pandemic-affected economy.[4]

According to Cyber Security Hub,[5] 75% of the cybersecurity practitioners surveyed answered 'phishing/social engineering attack' when asked, "What are the three most dangerous cyber security threats your organization faces today?" This was followed by supply chain/third-party risks at 36% and lack of cyber security expertise at 30%. Attackers are increasingly looking to exploit new technologies, work from home policies, and social networks for criminal purposes. In the same Cyber Security Hub report, when asked to consider their

---

[3] Annual Vulnerability Report – Risk Based Security, Inc., 2021.

[4] Annual Cyber Risk Analytics Report – Risk Based Security, Inc., 2021.

[5] CS Hub Mid-Year Market Report 2022.

organization's approach to cybersecurity over the past 12 months, 30% of the cybersecurity practitioners said their organizations have a high prioritization of cybersecurity. This means that 70% of the respondents do not feel their organization prioritizes cybersecurity. The continuing evolution of threat actors taking advantage of the ever-growing number of software vulnerabilities, no end in sight for remote working, lack of organizational cybersecurity focus, and the ongoing cybersecurity skills shortages have placed the role of CISO in the crosshairs at organizations across the globe.

Last but not least, the 'trusted' insider remains the most dangerous adversary for any CISO. The frequency and impact of insider-committed or assisted crime can be blamed on several factors, but the threat is predicted to increase in part because of the poor economy, the constant move toward ease of access to the organization's data, and the growing trend of allowing non-traditional worksites. A forever changing and growing threat landscape is a fundamental element of the nature of the CISO's role.

Challenges

As if the constantly evolving threat landscape is not challenging enough, most CISOs find themselves with limited resources and not reporting directly to top management. In 2021, the (ISC)^2 Cybersecurity Workforce Study stated that the *"global cybersecurity workforce needs to grow 65 percent to effectively defend organizations' critical assets."*[6] This makes a large and complex role even more daunting, and the CISO often needs to make risk trade-offs when deciding how to spend limited dollars or task scarce cyber expertise. Without a seat at the table with senior management, the CISO often makes risk trade-off decisions well above their pay grade. Risk decisions that should be made by senior management after understanding the potential impact on the business are often forced upon the CISO. As a CISO, you must be aware and be cautious when being forced to make business decisions outside of your purview.

Another substantial challenge for the CISO is the human element. Whether it's the lack of information security awareness or the innovation people display when trying to work around security controls to do their jobs, the human element remains a top CISO challenge. As tough as implementing new technology can be, nothing is as demanding as managing people during the implementation of new technology, amid organizational change, and when facing a never-yet-seen global crisis. Add to this an intensifying regulatory environment, world tensions, and global economic concerns and you begin to understand the challenges faced by the CISO. Returning to the Cyber Security Hub report from earlier, it's not surprising that 75% of cybersecurity practitioners reported phishing/social engineering attack as one of the top three most dangerous cybersecurity threats their organization faces today.

---

[6] The State of Cybersecurity Leadership and Readiness Survey, 2021, conducted by Navisite.

The satisfaction

The CISO is meant to drive all information security functions within an organization and effect change across the entire enterprise. The role provides the opportunity to have significant impact and influence on the security posture and ultimate success of the organization. As cyber crime continues on its path as a major national security concern, and compliance with new regulations and international standards pose greater threats to organizations, the CISO is expected to lead the company's strategy and response.

If you love a challenge, enjoy learning new skills, relish something new every day, desire to be a trusted advisor, enjoy teaching, and want to make a real difference to the safety and soundness of your organization, the CISO role has it all.

CHAPTER 2: THE TRADITIONAL CISO JOB DESCRIPTION

"Tradition becomes our security and when the mind is secure, it is in decay."

Jiddu Krishnamurti
Indian Philosopher

The position and title CISO refers to the person in an organization with an exclusive information security focus. The CISO is responsible for overseeing the overall corporate security strategy, security architecture, and security function. The scope of the role traditionally covers all implemented security technologies and services, including security applications, perimeter defenses, physical and logical access control, and access management for all employees, contractors, and visitors. As the organization's dedicated information security officer, this role also has enterprise-level responsibility for all data/information security policies, standards, evaluations, audits, and corporate security awareness programs.

The CISO works with user and technical groups as well as internal auditors in the development and implementation of a security strategy designed to provide a high level of security over information and information processing systems while preserving and enhancing system access and usability.

A typical CISO is responsible for directing the overall activities of the security function along with the following roles and functions:

- Define and implement an ongoing information security risk assessment program, which will define, identify, and classify critical assets, assess threats and vulnerabilities regarding those assets, and recommend safeguards
- Develop, implement, and manage the overall enterprise process for security strategy and associated architecture using security standards and best practice
- Develop and implement policies, standards, and guidelines related to information security
- Work with corporate executives, business managers, internal audit, and legal counsel to understand security and regulatory compliance requirements, and to map those requirements to current projects
- Oversee the continuous monitoring and protection of information and information systems
- Serve as the enterprise focal point for security incident response planning and execution
- Investigate and analyze suspected security breaches and recommend corrective actions
- Assist internal audit with developing appropriate criteria to assess the compliance of new/existing applications and technology with enterprise security standards and best practice
- Establish and monitor the analysis of the planned procurement of new applications, services, and technologies

- Oversee the development and implementation of a corporate information security awareness and training program
- Evaluate changes to the corporate environment for security impact and present findings to management
- Monitor threats, understand the risk they pose, and communicate those risks to the business and to the board

Unfortunately, the CISO generally reports to the CIO, legal counsel or Chief Financial Officer, and is often viewed as a technician and policy enforcer who is tasked with ensuring that the organization's networks, information, and information systems are secure. Often this places the CISO in a negative light when perceived by business managers as always saying 'no' or 'go-slow' to the implementation of new products and services.

Equally unfortunate, but sometimes necessary, the CISO must wear many hats depending on the size of the organization. Larger organizations normally have well-diversified roles at the C-suite, meaning the CISO can focus on information security and risk management. In small, less-funded organizations, the CISO will likely also handle the roles of Chief Security Officer, Chief Risk Officer, Compliance Officer, and/or Chief Privacy Officer.

Qualifications for the early established CISO position often read more like that of a subject matter expert then a senior manager:

- Awareness of and experience in:

- o Vulnerability testing and penetration testing
- o Standards-based architecture
- o Network-based security
- o Compliance monitoring and policy enforcement
- o Developing security practices
- A college degree (BA/BS), or equivalent work experience
- Certified Information Systems Security Professional (CISSP), Certified Information Security Manager (CISM), and/or Certified Information Systems Auditor (CISA)
- Results-oriented and commitment focused
- Excellent project management skills
- Business continuity planning, auditing, and vendor management experience
- Knowledge of pertinent regulations and laws

Although technical expertise remains a foundation requirement for the CISO role according to the hiring authority, to be truly effective and survive today, the CISO must be an articulate and persuasive leader with real business experience who can communicate security-related concepts to the senior management team to guide risk management decisions.

When applying for a CISO role, be very mindful of the defined requirements, expectations, and sometimes vague limitations. Focus not so much on the expected duties, but the defined reporting structure and expected involvement with top management allowing you to impact management decisions at the highest level.

The reporting hierarchy of the CISO signals how the organization views the cybersecurity function. Is it a role to tick a compliance checkbox? Is it a safety precaution subordinate to another function delivering products and services? Is it just another facet of the risk management function? Or, is the CISO viewed as a business enabler, focused on ensuring continuity and integrity of the organization's information security risk? Where the CISO reports is key to your success.

Chapter 3 will continue discussing the changing role of the CISO.

CHAPTER 3: THE CHANGING CISO ROLE

> *"Security can only be achieved through constant change, through discarding old ideas that have outlived their usefulness and adapting others to current facts."*
>
> **William O. Douglas**
> **Former Associate Justice of the Supreme Court of the United States**

The experience and skills that made yesterday's CISO successful no longer meet today's organizational needs. While still very much a technologist, today's CISO must have excellent communication and presentation skills, be able to understand everything as a process, and demonstrate keen business acumen. They need to be able to relate the adoption of new technology with the legal, regulatory, and business objectives in a way that management can use when making decisions about resource allocations and risk management.

While today's CISO must stay abreast of the latest in security technology, the role requirements go far beyond this. Managing information security has evolved into being more about the management of risk, business priorities, and compliance requirements, and monitoring the latest threats to the business. Today's CISO needs to be integrated into all aspects of the organization and have a full understanding of the business requirements, strategy, and objectives to do the job effectively and survive.

Today's CISO – Enlightened leader

Today's threat environment requires more than a security function coordinator. The successful CISO will not only fulfill the role of security leader but will also act as a connecting agent between functions to help executives see their common challenges. The CISO will accept the role of teacher and of helping to build these connections between departments to specifically address the challenges impacting security and operational risk. By virtue of their position, CISOs can not only add value and lead a business-enabling function but also provide the means for a competitive advantage for the organization.

The CISO as an enlightened leader realizes that organizations succeed by taking risks and the ones that fail do so because they didn't take the right risks or they didn't oversee the risk management process very well. CISOs need to consider risk from a business perspective and view each business function owner as a customer who requires help to innovate or deliver their product/service. The days of automatically saying no to any new idea that involved access to sensitive data, penetration of the security perimeter, or allowing mobile computing or remote access to data must be left behind. Today's new solutions are opportunities for the enlightened CISO to provide creative direction and influence to directly contribute to the overall revenue growth while ensuring information security for the organization is secure.

A large part of a CISO's job is to clearly articulate to everyone in the organization how security relates to business objectives. To be effective as the organizational communicator, the CISO must assume a variety of roles to reach all employees from the shop floor to the board room. The CISO must be prepared to play an enabling role during system development, by introducing security early, and by being accessible, approachable, responsive, and willing to be accountable throughout the product lifecycle.

Holistic security[7]

Even though CISOs frequently participate in related areas such as business continuity/disaster recovery planning, loss and fraud prevention, physical security, and employee safety in addition to information security and privacy, it is rare for the CISO to have full responsibility for these areas. In organizations that take an enlightened view of the total responsibilities placed on the security officer, the Chief Security Officer (CSO) has emerged as the executive responsible for the organization's entire corporate security posture including human resources, physical assets, and electronic assets.

There are a number of factors at work, not least of which is the growing motivation of CEOs and corporate boards to take a strategic and enterprise-wide view of business risk. Driven in part by regulations such as the Sarbanes–Oxley Act, Gramm–Leach–Bliley Act, Health Insurance Portability and Accountability Act, EU General Data Protection Regulation (GDPR), California Privacy Rights Act (CPRA), Cybersecurity Information Sharing Act (CISA), and Federal Information Security Modernization

---

[7] The holistic security momentum theory: Why resistance is futile, Derek Slater, April 15, 2005, CSO.

Act (FISMA), organizations realize the importance of data privacy and coordinating compliance activities to positively impact business objectives, internal operations, and external partner relationships, and, most importantly, satisfy customers.

In addition, the following technologies and business forces are taking hold that require a proactive and well-defined strategy from the CISO.

- **Internet of Things (IoT):** Sixty-one percent of organizations were using IoT in 2019 according to a report from Kaspersky[8]. Having a security strategy aimed at addressing this additional threat landscape will be paramount for the CISO.
- **Supply chain vulnerabilities:** The onslaught of software vulnerabilities mentioned in Chapter 1 means that the entire supply chain is at risk. When considering the risk to your software bill of materials (SBOM), all software must be under your security program.
- **Biometrics:** Fingerprints, facial recognition, retinal scan, voice, and even DNA are part of the growing use of biometrics for access control. With all the ease-of-use benefits, biometrics come with increased data storage requirements, privacy concerns, and regulatory risks if breached. CISOs must gain a

---

[8] Benefits and challenges of IoT in business – Kaspersky Lab, 2020.

working-level knowledge of this prevalent security technology.

- **Artificial Intelligence (AI):** Since OpenAI released ChatGPT in November 2022, many security experts predicted it would only be a matter of time before cyber criminals used the AI chatbot to write malware and enable other nefarious activities.[9] Just weeks after its release, ChatGPT was allowing bad actors with no coding experience to develop malware.[10] AI, for good and bad, needs to be a focus for CISOs.

- **Employees:** Always considered an organization's greatest asset, in recent years employees have earned the label of greatest security threat based on their inside knowledge and access to its most sensitive data. Today's employees remain a security threat, with an added facet that they are no longer loyal to the organization. Refusing to return to the office, quiet-quitting, and low unemployment rates all work to embolden the employee's label as the greatest threat to security.

In summary, CISOs are facing challenges from new technology, expanded threats from old threat actors, and

---

[9] *https://www.darkreading.com/omdia/chatgpt-artificial-intelligence-an-upcoming-cybersecurity-threat-*.
[10] Attackers Are Already Exploiting ChatGPT to Write Malicious Code – Dark Reading, Jai Vijayan, January 9, 2023.

an increasingly hostile environment brough on by unmotivated employees.

CHAPTER 4: THE NEW CISO'S TOOLBOX

"Tomorrow comes at us with ever-increasing speed. We need to engage it – today. Seize its opportunities – now. Start shaping its possibilities – in this very moment. And our approach must be very different from the behaviors we've relied on in the past."

Dr. Price Pritchett
Author and Management Consultant

According to the 2022 (ISC)^2 Cybersecurity Workforce Study, the cybersecurity workforce has reached an all-time high, with an estimated 4.7 million professionals. However, there's still a global shortage of 3.4 million workers in this field.[11] In spite of this labor challenge, there remains a chasm between what C-level managers say about the importance of cybersecurity and reality (only 7% of cybersecurity leaders report to the CEO).[12] CEO expectations with regard to the cybersecurity leader's ability to not only understand and align with business objectives but also to actively participate in achieving those objectives are not being met.

To narrow the chasm between expectations and reality, today's CISO cannot remain just a master technician assigned under another function. They need to develop the

---

[11] 2022 (ISC)^2 Cybersecurity Workforce Study.
[12] Security and the C-Suite: Making Security Priorities Business Priorities – LogRhythm, 2022.

skills of a leader, a facilitator, a communicator, and an agent of change worthy of a seat at the CEO's table. They also need to prepare to be a trusted adviser to senior management who can translate information security threats and business risk into terms that stakeholders can understand and relate to.

This chapter discusses the skills required of the new CISO to be this trusted adviser.

Let's begin by contrasting the labels used to describe the CISO of yesterday to the adjectives defining the new CISO (Table 1).

Table 1: Labels Used To Describe CISOs

Yesterday's CISO	New CISO
Subject matter expert	Trusted adviser
Analyst	Facilitator and leader
Technical risk expert	Risk manager
Individual contributor	Integrative business thinker
Chief Security Officer	Chief Risk Officer
Administrator	Strategist
Manager	Visionary

The most obvious contrast is that yesterday's CISO is singularly focused on individual expertise and all things technical while the new CISO's focus is on leadership, risk management, and business objectives.

How do we start the shift?

In short, CISOs need to break the stereotypes. The first, and possibly the most, ingrained stereotype is that security professionals don't understand business. Or at least they don't demonstrate any signs that they do. It appears to most senior managers that the only risk a CISO focuses on is loss, and never do they hear CISOs speak of the business benefits of taking risks to meet objectives.

The CISO's focus on the negative and the potential loss is expressed in terms few understand, like cyber forensics, intrusion prevention, and security patches, cause most managers to believe that CISOs have little interest in or understanding of business. The truth is there are few people in the organization in a better position to understand the business processes than the security professional. How else would a CISO know what needs protection, where to place the controls, and how to implement those security measures?

The issue, then, is that CISOs need to shift at least part of their attention to how to add increased value for clients and stakeholders without increasing the risk to the organization's assets. CISOs need not always be focused on decreasing risk. Sometimes increasing the potential of a positive outcome without increasing risk is what the business needs. Today's cybersecurity leader, the new

CISO, is in a great position to offer insight into how the organization can do just that.

What actions can you take today?

1. **Learn what keeps senior management up at night**: In the past, security professionals could mainly focus on regulatory compliance and corporate governance issues; however, today's CISO needs to be a trusted adviser as management seeks to balance risk aversion and value-creating behavior. Senior managers must focus on creating and sustaining business value. The CISO's job is to understand what this means to the organization and to proactively support their efforts. According to IBM's 2021 Institute for Business Value (IBV) CEO study,[13] CEOs are prioritizing employees' well-being, technology, and strong leadership to position their organizations for success post-pandemic. As a cybersecurity leader, you are in a unique position to help in these areas.

2. **Learn what your business competitors are doing**: One of the best ways to demonstrate your value to senior management is to discover and report on what technologies and initiatives your competitors have implemented or are considering. Consider all competitors, (direct, indirect, perceived, and

---

[13] Own your impact: Practical pathways to transformational sustainability – IBM Institute for Business Value, 2021.

aspirational), and analyze competitor content, social media, ads, trade shows, marketing and advertising industry and trade association publications, and industry research and business surveys.

3. **Look for ways new technology can benefit your business**: Technology is constantly changing. At any given time, a new product or an upgrade to an existing product could drastically alter the competitive landscape. Whether the new technology will improve customer service or allow you to be more price competitive, not being aware could place your organization's survival at risk. The actions required to discover the innovations are simple and straightforward. The discipline to persevere is the challenge. Make it a habit to scan online news articles about computers, telephones, wireless networking, AI, biometrics, software, and consumer-focused technology. Take note of your surroundings and especially the technology used by young people.

4. **Learn how to speak business**: The days of the security guru hanging out in the data center without face-to-face contact with management are over. Not only do CISOs need to come out from the dark but they also need to be able to speak a language management can understand. Remember: Senior managers are interested in broad business issues like long-term corporate strategy and how to increase revenue, profitability, and market share. Being able

to relate your goals and objectives to a business-focused value proposition is critical to any C-level executive listening to you. Although polishing your group presentation skills will always come in handy, you need to be able to explain easily how your security-based initiatives align to the business goals. Define the way your initiatives support their objectives and be ready to interject when appropriate. Listen to how non-technical managers talk to one another and avoid using security jargon whenever possible.

5. **Dress for your audience**: This means dress to fit in with the people you are addressing, which could mean a suit, business casual, weekend casual, or something in between. A suit won't help when you are trying to make a point to 20-somethings; jeans and a T-shirt will detract from your message when presenting to the board. Always inquire about the appropriate and proper dress and don't take a flimsy answer from the organizer. There are numerous reasons for the poor communication between security professionals and management; don't let your appearance be one of them. Avoid jumping from ripped jeans and a T-shirt to a suit; everyone will think you have a job interview. Start slowly by going to the next level of dress over weeks. Dockers and a golf shirt with a collar, followed by dress slacks and a short-sleeve dress

shirt and then to a suit. You are looking to fit in with the level you want to influence.

6. **Write for your audience**: Just like you need to dress for your audience, you need to write appropriately, too. It may be perfectly acceptable to come straight to the point using technical jargon and abbreviations when writing to your security colleagues, but when communicating with management you need to know how they think and how they prefer to be briefed. When writing to a C-level executive, think business journal. Articles in the world's best business newspapers say it all in the first lines of each article. If you want more details, you read on; if not, you can stop and still know the key points. You need to learn how to write as if your article were being published in the *Wall Street Journal*, *The Times* of London, or *The Globe and Mail*. Think of it as starting with the conclusion and then providing the details to back it up. Don't count on management reading through your entire thought process to reach the conclusion. It's not how they think.

7. **Make yourself known outside your organization**: No matter how little your senior management team seems to know what you do all day, the moment your name or your organization's name is mentioned positively in print or at a management gathering, they will care a lot. Consider setting yourself up on LinkedIn and X (formerly known as Twitter) and

freely share your areas of expertise. Contact organizations that set up conferences and volunteer to speak. Start a blog about one of your passions and update it regularly. Look for opportunities to volunteer your time and talents in your field of expertise. Jump at every chance to meet new people because the more people you meet, the more people will know you, and the better your chances are of finding an opportunity to bring favorable press to you and your organization.

8. **Think holistically about your job**: In organizations that take an enlightened view of the CISO role, the CISO is the executive responsible for the organization's entire corporate security posture, including both physical and electronic. At the tactical level, technology is increasingly being infused into physical security tools; at the strategic level, CEOs and corporate boards are looking for one go-to person for both advisory services and guidance during times of crisis. The new CISO needs to prepare for this role.

CHAPTER 5: RISK MANAGEMENT

> *"Good risk management fosters vigilance in times of calm and instills discipline in times of crisis."*
>
> **Dr. Michael Ong**
> **Executive Director, Center for Financial Markets**

This chapter is about the heart of any ISMS: the risk management methodology. The methodology used to identify, analyze, evaluate, and treat risks is foundational to any ISMS, and sets the stage for identifying and appropriately protecting the organization's assets.

Before we begin, what would you say is the definition of risk? Most security professionals would quote something like this:

1. Risk is the impact to an asset considering the probability that a particular threat will exploit a particular information system vulnerability.
2. Risk is the potential that a given threat will exploit vulnerabilities to cause loss or damage to an asset.
3. Risk is the combination of the consequence of an event and the probability of the event happening.

The preferable definition that can be used to teach information security risk management concepts to senior management is an extension to point 3 above.

Risk is defined as the consequence of an event *multiplied* by the probability of the event occurring.

Consequence is further defined as the impact to the organization from a breach of confidentiality, integrity, or availability. Probability is defined by two parts: the probability of the threat occurring and the probability of exposure to the threat.

In other words, consequence is defined as the Asset Value (AV), the probability of the threat occurring as the Threat Likelihood (TL), and the probability of exposure to the threat as the Vulnerability Exposure (VE).

The definition of risk then becomes:

Risk = AV × (TL × VE), where AV is the consequence and (TL × VE) is the probability.

Note: Asset Value (AV) has little to do with an asset's cost or financial calculations. An asset's value to the organization is a relative measure of the impact to the organization that could be caused if that asset was breached.

Breaking down the risk equation into these three distinct elements helps both security practitioners and business owners understand the risk assessment process and to do a better job of estimating the relative ratings[14] for each element. Helping the business owners understand the risk assessment process provides accuracy, credibility, and repeatability to the process. Remember: The objective of calculating risk scores is to identify the appropriate

---

[14] A qualitative scale of 1–5 is commonly used to rate each element using definitions relevant to the organization for each number on the scale.

allocation of your organization's limited resources to mitigate the highest risk to your most 'valued' assets.

Risk = AV (1–5) × TL (1–5) × VE (1–5).

The organization's highest risk score would equal 5 x 5 x 5 = 125, and would warrant early mitigation actions to lower the risk score.

One of the best descriptions of an organizationally appropriate risk assessment approach is in the International Standard, ISO/IEC 27001:2022 (*Information security, cybersecurity and privacy protection – Information security management systems – Requirements*).[15]

What does ISO/IEC 27001:2022 have to say about risk assessment?

ISO/IEC 27001:2022 (ISO 27001) is an internationally recognized information security standard that provides management and technical compliance requirements against which organizations and professionals can be certified. ISO 27001 guides organizations to establish, implement, maintain, and improve an ISMS that assures the confidentiality, integrity, availability, and privacy of information. ISO 27001 comprises two major sections: the management system requirements defined in paragraphs 4 through 10, and the security controls defined in Annex A

---

[15] ISO/IEC 27001:2022 (*Information security, cybersecurity and privacy protection – Information security management systems – Requirements*) – International Organization for Standardization.

of the Standard. While organizations have the right to select only the controls applicable to their operations from Annex A, excluding any of the requirements defined in paragraphs 4 through 10 is unacceptable if an organization claims compliance with ISO 27001.

To be compliant with ISO 27001, an organization must demonstrate the establishment and use of a risk assessment methodology that is suited to the business considering information security as well as legal and regulatory requirements. Clauses 6.1.2 and 6.1.3 of ISO 27001 define the necessary and critical elements of a risk assessment methodology.

The risk assessment approach must also define the criteria for accepting risks and identifying acceptable levels of risk. The Standard also provides the framework for conducting risk assessments, risk analysis, and risk treatment, leading to the selection of the proper security controls from Annex A.

The necessary steps within a risk assessment framework include the following:

1. Identifying the organization's **assets and the owners** of the assets. This is all about knowing what you need to protect within the scope of the ISMS and who is responsible.
2. Calculating the **impacts** or AVs that a loss of confidentiality, integrity, and/or availability of the assets may have on the organization.
3. Identifying the **threats** and TL to the assets.

4. Identifying the **vulnerabilities** that are most likely paired with each threat to determine the VE.
5. A risk score can now be calculated for each asset and its threat and vulnerability pairs.

With the completion of this step, the organization can prioritize the risks it faces, make a conscious decision to accept individual risks, or set priorities around implementing security controls to mitigate the highest risks.

The risk methodology selected does not have to be complex, expensive, or over-reaching; it must, however, ensure the risk assessments produce comparable and reproducible results.

Risk treatment plans

With the risks to the organization more fully understood, a CISO is now ready to evaluate the options for the treatment of risks. Possible actions could include:

- Avoiding risks, by not performing the activity that creates the risk
- Knowingly accepting risks (based on risk acceptance criteria)
- Transferring the associated risks to other parties like suppliers or insurers
- Applying appropriate security controls

If applying a security control is the preferred action in the treatment of a risk, Annex A provides a comprehensive list of security controls that are commonly relevant in most organizations. Of course, the list is not exhaustive, and organizations are encouraged to add controls as needed.

As you can see, implementing a security control is just one of four potential risk treatments. It is the established and operating risk assessment methodology that enables an organization to make informed decisions about the uncertainty involved in accomplishing its objectives. The concept of risk *assessment* defined in ISO 27001 has been expanded to risk *management* in the international standard ISO 31000:2018.[16] The next section discusses the major concepts within ISO 31000:2018.

ISO 31000:2018: Risk management – Principles and guidelines

Originally released in 2009, the international standard ISO 31000:2009 provided principles and generic guidelines on risk management. It was meant to be used by any public, private, or community enterprise, association, group, or individual, and can be applied to any type of risk.

The 2018 version, ISO 31000:2018 (ISO 31000), defines risk as the *"effect of uncertainty on objectives."* Notice that the definition's focus is on the *"effect"* of *"uncertainty"* on the achievement of an organization's objectives and not on a single event.

The *"effect"* is parallel to the asset value or impact to the organization in the definition above, and *"uncertainty"*

---

[16] ISO 31000:2018 (*Risk management – guidelines*) – International Organization for Standardization.

can be thought of in terms of threat likelihood and vulnerability exposure. The real insight offered in ISO 31000 comes with the notion that the consequence of uncertainty can not *only* involve loss, non-compliance, and harm but *also* benefit and advantage to the organization.

Risk management principles according to ISO 31000:2018

According to ISO 31000, for risk management to be effective, an organization should at all levels comply with the following eight principles:

1. **"Integrated** – Risk management is integrated into the organization's processes. Risk management is an integral part of all organizational processes [not a standalone activity, but part of management's responsibilities].

2. **Structured and comprehensive** – Risk management is structured and comprehensive. Risk management is systematic, structured, comprehensive, and timely [provides consistent, comparable, and reliable results].

3. **Customized** – Risk management is customized to your organization. Risk management is tailored [aligned with the organization's external and internal context and risk profile].

4. **Inclusive** – Risk management is inclusive and transparent. Risk management is transparent and inclusive [open involvement at all levels assures that

all views are taken into account when determining risk criteria].

5. **Dynamic** – Risk management is dynamic, fluid, and responsive to change. Risk management is dynamic, iterative, and responsive to change [continually sensitive to and responding to change].

6. **Best-available information** – Risk management takes into consideration the best-available information. Risk management is based on the best-available information [historical data, experience, stakeholder feedback, observation, threat intelligence, forecasts, and expert judgment].

7. **Human factors and culture** – Risk management takes into account human factors and the company culture. Risk management takes human and cultural factors into account [recognizes capabilities, perceptions, and intentions of both internal and external people important to the process].

8. **Continual improvement** – Risk management encourages and drives continual improvement. Risk management facilitates continual improvement of the organization [implement strategies to improve risk management maturity]."

Although ISO 31000 can be applied throughout an organization, the design and implementation of your organization's risk management framework will need to take into account its particular objectives, context, structure, operations, processes, functions, projects, products, services, and assets, and specific practices employed.

Risk management – The heart of information security

The right-sized, organization-appropriate risk management process will help you maximize the potential benefits and select the controls necessary to protect your business while producing repeatable and comparable results to measure the effectiveness of your risk management process.

Taking the perspective that cybersecurity leaders need to think and behave like 'business owners,' a CISO needs to not only implement a certified, living, breathing risk management methodology but also must encourage the organization to only do business with other companies that do the same to ensure the appropriate security controls are in place throughout the supply chain.

Information security has never really been just about IT security controls. IT is only a part of the information security challenge, just as information security is only a part of the larger issue of risk management – protecting and ensuring the life and health of the organization. The business of risk management is far too important to be left to any single department. Failure to manage information security risks has serious and far-reaching effects, including:

- Threatening the continuity of operations
- Eroding the bottom line
- Depressing the value of the organization
- Compromising future earnings

- Destroying an organization's reputation and image
- Substantial financial penalties and even jail time

What differentiates successful CISOs and their information security strategies from the not-so-successful appears to be a strategic and comprehensive risk management focus, rather than just reacting to security incidents one by one. Successful CISOs assure that their organizations have a defined risk management methodology that systematically identifies and evaluates uncertainty before security controls are selected and implemented. Identification and valuation of the organization's most valued assets and understanding the uncertainty surrounding those assets, along with the consequences of a security failure, is the best way to guide the appropriation of limited resources.

To lead, not just encourage, organizations to establish this framework, CISOs need to accelerate a change in focus away from technical security controls to an overall enterprise risk management methodology.

CHAPTER 6: THE INFORMATION SECURITY MANAGEMENT SYSTEM

> *"The problem is never how to get new, innovative thoughts into your mind, but how to get the old ones out."*
>
> **Dee Hock**
> **Creator of Visa**

In spite of the views of many CISOs, securing an organization's information assets has never really been *just* about implementing technical security controls. The role of the traditional CISO within the typical IT department can play only a small part in solving the information security challenge. Implementing technical security controls defined by the CISO is only a part of the larger issue of risk management. Today's CISO needs to adopt, promote, and lead the implementation of an ISMS designed to protect the organization's information assets and ensure the life and health of the business. ISO 27001 defines the management system required for today's threat environment.

This chapter is not another general tutorial describing the background, history, and security objectives defined in ISO 27001. Nor is it focused on the 93 best-practice security controls listed in Annex A of the Standard. Instead, this chapter discusses the elements of a living, breathing ISMS defined in ISO 27001 and the benefits of implementation and third-party certification.

Elements of an Information Security Management System

ISO 27001 provides a model for establishing, implementing, maintaining, and continually improving an ISMS that should be scaled in accordance with the needs of the organization. The design and implementation of the ISMS follows a process approach and should address the organization's needs and objectives, external and internal issues, security requirements, the processes employed, and the size and structure of the organization.

The Standard no longer calls out the use of the Plan-Do-Check-Act (PDCA) model (also known as the Shewhart Cycle or the Deming Wheel) to guide the development and implementation of the ISMS processes. The management system requirements listed still do, however, define many of the very same actions to implement an ISMS:

- **Context of the Organization (Plan):**
  To establish the ISMS, the CISO must understand the organization's information assets, external and internal issues, and the needs and expectations of interested parties. Boundaries, security requirements applicability, and interfaces and dependencies with other organizations must be defined to establish the ISMS scope. Document the risk assessment and create the policies, objectives, processes, and procedures relevant to managing risk and improving information security to deliver results in accordance

with the organization's overall business strategy objectives.

- **Do (implement and operate the ISMS)**:
  Implement and operate the ISMS policy, procedures, processes, and controls developed during the Plan phase to manage the organization's information security risks within the context of its overall business risk.

- **Check (monitor and review the ISMS)**:
  Monitor and, where applicable, assess process performance against ISMS policy, objectives, and practical experience, and report the results to management for review to measure the performance and effectiveness of the ISMS.

- **Act (maintain and improve the ISMS)**:
  Take corrective and preventive actions, based on the results of the internal ISMS audit program and management review or other relevant information, to achieve continual improvement of the ISMS processes and implemented security controls.

Key processes within an Information Security Management System

The processes defined within ISO 27001 describe a methodology to properly identify an organization's information assets, the threats and vulnerabilities to those assets, and the necessary controls to assure the security of those assets, and to make sure the implemented controls are effective. But, most of all, ISO 27001 defines a management system to establish processes, policies, and procedures relevant to managing risk and improving information security in accordance with the organization's overall business strategy. A management system is much more than a list of security controls, even if they are "best practice."

Key management system processes include:

Plan phase

- Document management's commitment to provide resources to establish, implement, maintain, and continually improve the ISMS
- Understand the organization's information assets and external and internal issues, and the needs and expectations of interested parties
- Understand the boundaries, security requirements applicability, and interfaces and dependencies with other organizations within the ISMS scope
- Establish a framework for setting security objectives and the overall direction and principles for action
- Define the risk assessment approach and methodology of the organization
- Select controls for the treatment of risks
- Obtain management approval of the proposed residual risks to implement and operate the ISMS
- Establish document control procedures

Do phase

- Formulate a risk treatment plan that identifies the appropriate management action, resources, responsibilities, and priorities for managing information security risks
- Implement the risk treatment plan to achieve the identified control objectives
- Define how to measure the effectiveness of the selected controls or groups of controls
- Implement training and awareness programs
- Manage the operation of the ISMS
- Manage resources for the ISMS
- Ensure all personnel assigned responsibilities defined in the ISMS are competent to perform the required tasks
- Implement procedures and other controls capable of enabling prompt detection of and response to security events

Check phase

- Execute monitoring and reviewing procedures and other controls
- Undertake regular reviews of the effectiveness of the ISMS
- Measure the effectiveness of controls to verify that security requirements and risk reduction goals have been met

- Review risk assessments at planned intervals and review the residual risks and the identified acceptable levels of risks
- Conduct internal ISMS audits at planned intervals
- Undertake a management review of the ISMS on a regular basis
- Update security plans to take into account the findings of monitoring and reviewing activities
- Record actions and security events that could have an impact on the effectiveness or performance of the ISMS

Act phase

- Take appropriate corrective and preventive actions
- Implement the identified improvements in the ISMS
- Communicate the actions and improvements to all interested parties
- Ensure that the improvements achieve their intended objectives

The real power of ISO 27001 comes from embracing the elements of the management system and not just implementing a list of security controls. When an organization implements an ISO 27001-compliant ISMS, not only does it safeguard assets through best-practice security controls but it also more importantly empowers the organization with a management framework and risk assessment methodology that assures the proper recognition and treatment of all risks to the business.

Whether the risk comes in the form of data privacy legislation, legal or regulatory actions, theft, IT failures, natural disasters, terrorism, hacking, or malicious employees, the risk assessment methodology and management system will guide the organization to identify the proper risk treatment. The ISMS allows the organization to be ever responsive to new risks and to address each risk in a manner most suitable to the organization at the time. This means that when you have a well-structured risk assessment framework, you can not only minimize negative impact from threats but also maximize positive impact from opportunities.

A well-implemented control may provide security for a time, but a well-established management system and risk assessment methodology will provide the means for an organization to protect itself at all times.

The case for ISO/IEC 27001:2022 certification

Seeking third-party certification against the ISO 27001 standard is a powerful step for an organization toward effecting and demonstrating compliance with internationally recognized best practices in information security. The Standard provides an organization with a continuous protection methodology, allowing a flexible, effective, and defensible approach to security and privacy compliance.

The most powerful aspect of certification is being able to demonstrate to customers, employees, suppliers, and business partners the validated existence of a fully operational risk assessment methodology and management system.

The international mutual recognition certification scheme for ISO 27001 makes it the touchstone for effective, comprehensive, and verifiable information security management practices. There are many benefits derived from certification, but a few of the most noteworthy include:

- Credibility and trust with stakeholders, partners, citizens, and customers
- Documented operational, productivity, and quality improvements
- Certified once, accepted globally
- A holistic, risk-based approach to compliance
- Reduced business disruption from ongoing customer assessments
- Demonstrated security status according to internationally accepted criteria
- Demonstrated due diligence in complying with SOX, HIPAA, GLBA and 21 CFR Part 11.

ISO 27001 certification assures clients, employees, suppliers, business partners, and future customers that your organization has a continuous protection methodology, allowing a flexible, effective, and defensible approach to security and privacy compliance. This is far more effective than a list of implemented security controls that may or may not be needed or appropriate.

To summarize the importance of risk assessment in information security, it's all about the risk assessment framework and management system that guides an organization through the process of identifying and protecting the organization's most valuable assets. It's not about the technology and it's not about aimlessly implementing security controls, even if they are "best practice." As an organization's CISO, you need to not only understand this but also live it every day.

CHAPTER 7: CISO SURVIVAL

> *"Learning is not compulsory ... neither is survival."*
>
> **W. Edwards Deming**
> **American Engineer and Statistician**

CISOs are bombarded with new challenges every day. In a single week, a CISO can be called upon to recommend security applications, build security awareness, be a risk manager, be a consultant to management, lead incident response, be an advocate for business innovation, be a strategic thinker, and establish and support top management security champions.

The role includes developing, articulating, and delivering an IT security and risk management strategy that is aligned with business objectives. The scope of the role is wide and includes technology deployment, strategy and communications, risk management, security operations, investigations/incident response, security awareness training, and business continuity planning/disaster recovery.

There are a number of skills and competencies that a CISO must possess and demonstrate on a daily basis to earn and maintain organizational credibility to meet the latest business challenges.

A solid foundation

To truly execute the role at a high and sustained level, the CISO must maintain a combination of both hard and soft skills. The role requires not only understanding information security and risk management but also mastering competence in three foundational areas: education and certifications; relevant experience; and soft skills including personal qualities, habits, attitudes, and social graces.

Education and certifications:

With a large majority of information assets being electronic, a technical education and/or an in-depth understanding of how the organization's information is created, processed, and stored is essential. Ideally, the CISO would have a degree in IT or information security combined with a business degree. It should be noted that ISACA's 2022 State of Cybersecurity survey found that the trend of requiring a university degree for entry-level cybersecurity positions is reversing, with a smaller percentage of enterprises requiring university degrees. Short of the ideal formal education, a law or business degree combined with a deep understanding of security industry frameworks, approaches, and standards such as ISO/IEC 27001:2022, COBIT®, NIST 800-53, or ITIL® would be valuable.

Continual education is a hallmark of today's successful CISO. Vendor-neutral certifications, including CISSP, CISM, and CISA demonstrate knowledge, refresh previous training, invoke innovative thinking, and increase internal and external credibility. The ISACA State of Cybersecurity survey also found that 89% of respondents require security credentials, 95% are seeking prior hands-on cybersecurity experience, and 81% are looking for hands-on training when determining whether a candidate is qualified. While industry certifications proved important in qualifying for a cybersecurity position, the survey reports that soft skills and Cloud-computing skills are the top two skill gaps among today's cybersecurity professionals.[17]

Relevant experience:

Having a documented hands-on track record in successfully developing a security program, implementing security controls, and responding to a security incident goes a long way toward preparing the security professional for the CISO role. With an understanding of the management side of business and what it takes to support business objectives, the CISO will find themselves in great demand. Business management experience ensures the CISO has a firm understanding of the potential impact decisions and recommendations may have on the organization's security/risk posture, operational cost, efficiency, and ability to respond to customer demands. If you understand the organization, its functions and processes, you have a higher success rate in predicting the security weaknesses that may be in play or introduced when deploying new products or services.

Involvement in industry events, associations, and security forums is also an important aspect of a CISO's experience. Active participation outside the organization

---

[17] State of Cybersecurity 2022, Global Update on Workforce Efforts, Resources and Cyberoperations – ISACA.

provides a vehicle for sharing experiences with other CISOs to explore how they have tackled common problems, deployed technology, and addressed the latest security threats. Although the CISO needs to spend time 'in the office' to protect the organization's assets, it helps to 'get out' to remain up to speed with the continually changing threat landscape and developments in the world of technology.

Soft skills:

There is an axiom in the business world that suggests that hard skills (education, certifications, and years of experience) can get you an interview, but it's your soft skills that get you the job offer. So what are 'soft skills' and which ones are important for today's CISO? Soft skills refer to your personal qualities, habits, attitudes, and social graces that make you compatible with the organization's values. Although all organizations may not value the same set of soft skills, it is the combination of both hard and soft skills that will enable you to perform well.

When looking for a CISO position, or to further your advancement in the role, your soft skills are every bit as vital to your success as education and experience. Some of the most lacking soft skills in cybersecurity candidates[18] include:

---

[18] State of Cybersecurity 2022, Global Update on Workforce Efforts, Resources and Cyberoperations – ISACA.

Communication skills:

Good communication skills mean that you are articulate and a good listener. You can make your case and express your thoughts in a way that builds bridges with colleagues, customers, and vendors. The maturity of your communication skills has a direct bearing on your professional image and potential to influence. Organizations place a high value on employees with polished communication skills. The art of effective communication does not depend on impressive words or flashy emails. Rather, it is reflected in your ability to get a point across as concisely, politely, and clearly as possible.

Critical thinking[19]:

Critical thinking is the intellectually disciplined process of actively and skillfully conceptualizing, applying, analyzing, synthesizing, and/or evaluating information gathered from, or generated by, observation, experience, reflection, reasoning, or communication, as a guide to belief and action. In its exemplary form, it is based on universal intellectual values that transcend subject matter divisions: clarity, accuracy, precision, consistency, relevance, sound evidence, good reasons, depth, breadth, and fairness.

---

[19] Critical thinking as defined by the National Council for Excellence in Critical Thinking, 1987.

Problem-solving skills:

Problem solving occurs when solutions are identified and implemented to resolve a gap or remove obstacles between our present situation and a desired goal. Problem solving generally includes the following steps: problem recognition, investigation and analysis, solution brainstorming, option analysis, and decision selection.

Team player:

Successful CISOs will be comfortable working as part of a team. It is important to fit in with and get along with other employees for the organization to run smoothly. Being a team player is not about being liked by everyone, nor does it mean you like everyone on the team. A true team player is an employee who can be counted on to do their part of the work, be relied on to complete tasks, and work cooperatively with others.

Strong work ethic[20]:

A strong work ethic is a set of values based on commitment and diligence. The characteristics of a strong work ethic can be described in four words:

1. **Desire:** How important is it to accomplish goals?
2. **Dedication:** Turning desire into action and lasting commitment to goals.

---

[20] Building a Strong Work Ethic, F. Scott Addis, January 2010 – Moneywatch.com.

3. **Determination:** Represents the intensity with which a person is dedicated to the accomplishment of goals.
4. **Discipline:** Staying with the strategy to achieve goals.

Positive attitude:

A positive attitude means to keep a set of ideas, values, and thoughts that tend to look for the good, to overcome problems, and to find the opportunities in every situation. A positive attitude helps you cope more easily with the daily challenges of both work and life. Adopted as a way of life, a positive attitude brings optimism and constructive change, and makes it easier to avoid negative thinking. A positive attitude is a state of mind that is well worth developing.

Time management abilities:

Time management skills boil down to awareness, organization, and commitment. Awareness comes from knowing and recording everything you are committed to doing. Organization is the ability to translate those goals into actionable tasks, and commitment is the follow-through to get the tasks complete. Time management skills are learnable abilities that recognize and solve personal and business problems.

Self-confidence:

Self-confidence is essentially an attitude that allows us to have a positive and realistic perception of ourselves and our abilities. It is characterized by personal attributes such as optimism, enthusiasm, affection, pride, independence, trust, assertiveness, the ability to handle criticism, and emotional maturity. Self-confidence is a deserved belief in your abilities without cockiness. Self-confidence projects a sense of calm, and inspires confidence and courage in others to ask questions and to freely contribute ideas.

Flexibility/adaptability[21]:

Successful CISOs live in the moment. Gallup Consulting defines those having adaptability as a strength as people who don't see the future as a fixed destination. Instead, you see it as a place created out of the choices that are made today. Adaptability enables you to respond willingly to the demands of the moment even if they pull you away from your plans. At heart, CISOs must be very flexible people who can stay productive when the demands of work are pulling in many different directions at once.

Calm under pressure:

Staying calm under pressure leads to clear thinking, better decisions, and an overall healthier work and personal life. Being able to handle the stress that accompanies conflicts, deadlines, and emergencies is a great asset to any CISO.

Your strategy to survive and prosper

To survive as a CISO, you need to have a daily plan that reminds you of the 'right' things to be thinking about (see Chapter 8), and a strategy that demonstrates your

---

[21] GALLUP Management Journal, Adaptability, September 12, 2002.

capability to be a trusted adviser to management while you deliver measurable results and maintain security at your organization.

There are six key principles[22] that a CISO should focus on:

1. **Build relationships within the organization**:
   CISOs need to develop relationships with key stakeholders long before contacting them to perform an assessment or to ask for money. A demonstrated understanding of the organization's processes, politics, expectations, concerns, and goals is essential.

2. **Focus initiatives on business goals**:
   Produce security strategies that support the business strategy and objectives to produce products and services. This will better ensure business owner and management buy-in and sponsorship.

3. **Link initiatives and plan**:
   Connect the business objectives with the requirements and challenges facing information security – threat environment, regulatory compliance, resource constraints, and technology deployment. Using these connections, map the next 12–18 months, displaying how the security initiatives

---

[22] What makes a CISO employable? Avtar Sehmbi, July 20, 2010 – Infosecurity (UK).

support what the organization is trying to achieve strategically and tactically.

4. **Deliver service**:

Staff managers often forget who their customers really are. They don't realize they need to sell themselves by focusing on quality service, presentation, punctuality, physical appearance, and credibility. Adding value to the organization is the goal of every engagement you have with management. Articulate cost reductions, return on investment, and risk reduction whenever possible.

5. **Professional credibility**:

To be a trusted adviser to top management, you need to build your professional capabilities and accomplishments. Stay connected to and seek recognition from the larger security community. Distribute informative industry white papers, relevant case studies, information security alerts, regulation overviews, and best-practice summaries. Deliver top management and board-level information security and risk management training whenever possible.

6. **Surround yourself with excellence**:

If you want to be excellent, you need to surround yourself with excellence. The CISO role is no different. Great CISOs surround themselves with great people who force them to be on their toes and to strive to be better. Don't fall into the trap of only hiring people who won't challenge you. If you do, your challenge may well be just keeping your job.

Historically, the typical CISO had a background in technical security/consulting or IT operations management. As regulatory compliance and new laws became a larger part of the CISO landscape, people from the legal profession and senior business managers joined the specialty. Regardless of their background, a CISO's longevity is not just about having the right qualifications (hard skills), but complementing them with both the soft skills discussed above and a well-executed survival strategy.

CHAPTER 8: SUMMARY – YOU BECOME WHAT YOU THINK ABOUT

> *"A man is but the product of his thoughts, what he thinks, he becomes."*
>
> **Mohandas Gandhi**
> **Indian Lawyer and Political Ethicist**

The concept is far from new; its truth is self-evident and it has never been more relevant. A more recent rendition of the concept is from the renowned author and speaker Earl Nightingale, who says, *"You become what you think about."* If this is the first time you have heard this phrase, let it sink in. It may not change your life in some lightning-strike way, but if you give it a chance you will recognize that you are surely becoming what you find yourself thinking about. Making a conscious effort to think about what you want to become can have a powerful impact on your job effectiveness and your success in life, if you think about the right things.

What do great CISOs think about today?

For starters, don't even think about looking at a traditional CISO job description. All you will find are overly technical requirements and the occasional high-level responsibility clause for the organization's security program. Neither are well suited to establishing you as a trusted adviser to senior management.

To define what great CISOs should be thinking about, let's remember the challenges facing today's CEO. In the C-Suite Challenge 2021: Leading in a Post-COVID-19

Recovery[23], it is no surprise that what CEOs view as their greatest challenges do not specifically focus on information security. The C-Suite Challenge 2021 reflects the following challenges that align well with what a great CISO should be thinking about:

- COVID-19-related disruptions
- Lack of quality talent
- Resource constraints relative to business needs
- Lack of an innovation culture
- Regulation
- Underleveraged use of data to grow
- Lack of data analytical skills
- Siloed internal structures
- Commitment to current business model
- Legacy technologies
- Unwillingness to change
- Employees resist change

In support of business objectives, a great CISO would focus on the following:

- Business projects require security to manage the organization's risk.
- Support everyone who builds products, delivers services, or sells either one.
- Technology's role is to support business objectives.

---

[23] C-Suite Challenge 2021: Leading in a Post-COVID-19 Recovery, March 2021 – The Conference Board.

- Business is the art of managing risk and I am the master of risk.
- Work on a daily basis to make C-level executives risk management disciples.
- Technology enables innovation and creativity.
- Explain everything in terms of risk levels so that people can understand.
- Security is every employee's job. Teach them what they need to know.

Protecting our greatest assets

In the past, technology has been the IT department's stronghold on the rest of the organization. The IT department used to be the first adopter of new technology and the first to explore the value of the latest hardware and software upgrades. Today, the IT department finds itself trying to catch up with and even slow down employees already using the latest in smartphones, social networking, instant messaging, and wireless applications. It seems the 'users' are not waiting for the IT department to introduce the new technology. They are not waiting for the CISO to bless the technology as 'safe' for use within the organization. Employees have become increasingly more tech-savvy and are willing to remain connected to their jobs at all hours of the day. Employees want to merge their work and personal technology. The expression "Employees are an organization's greatest asset" is as true today as ever before. Employees can also be an organization's greatest threat. The great CISO will take steps to both recognize and mitigate this fact.

What will great CISOs think about tomorrow?

Great CISOs recognize that the serious and ever-changing nature of today's security threats demand a strategic-minded response and not just an operational reaction to the latest headlines. This is a drastic change from being a working security coordinator to that of an evangelist of risk management, innovation through technology, and information security within the organization. Identifying threats, defining security controls, developing security architecture, overseeing planned mitigations, and monitoring the organization's security posture will always remain a CISO's responsibility, but the great CISO will also be thinking about how to attain business objectives through enabling technology while properly managing risk.

Future CISOs will need to develop the ability to think about information security and risk at the enterprise level and not just from the IT perspective. An enterprise view of information security, business continuity, compliance, safety, and physical security, and the ability to understand how it all impacts risk are crucial for tomorrow's CISO.

Every great CISO will ask themselves the following questions:

- How do I create a risk-aware culture?
- How do I advance information security and risk management into the business strategy?
- How do I communicate risk to stakeholders and become a trusted adviser to the executive team?

- How do I educate and collaborate on security and compliance issues?
- What information security strategy will keep us ahead of the bad guys?

How do you start thinking about the right things?

The secret to help you free your thinking is to take a sideways step and look at your position in the organization from the purview of senior management. Stop trying to desperately think of new technology projects that might inspire you and start considering what you can do to meet the organization's business challenges.

Especially in a challenging economic climate, management is looking for more ways to achieve business objectives and is not as interested in focusing solely on information security and regulatory compliance. The challenge for you is to break out of the mindset that taking on risk only has a negative component.

The CISO of yesterday rarely, if ever, deviates from their 'risk avoidance at all costs' mentality. If you want to be perceived as a valuable member of the team, it may be time to rethink your message. We will be living in a much different financial world for the next five to ten years. The traditional method of thinking and operating used to influence senior management in the past must now undergo a radical shift to reflect the realities of the current economic environment. More than ever before, you must know how to communicate effectively with senior management to compete for the organization's limited resources.

Earl Nightingale encourages us to complete a 30-day challenge[24] where you intentionally manage what you think about. His suggestion is to carry a card in your pocket that contains the key thoughts that you want to take hold and look at it throughout the day.

On one side of the card you write:

- You become what you think about
- Ask, and it shall be given to you
- Seek, and you shall find
- Knock, and it shall be opened unto you

On the other side of the card you could write:

- I am a trusted adviser to senior management.
- I will focus on helping people build products, deliver services, and increase sales.
- I will manage risk while maximizing positive outcomes.
- I will use technology to enable innovation and creativity.
- I will look for ways to build collaboration on security and compliance issues.

Create your own card today and carry it with you. Look at it several times a day and especially when you feel yourself slipping back into your old way of thinking. Try it for 30 days and watch how *"You become what you think about"* – a great CISO.

---

[24] The Strangest Secret, Earl Nightingale, September 12, 2006.

FURTHER READING

IT Governance Publishing (ITGP) is the world's leading publisher for governance and compliance. Our industry-leading pocket guides, books, training resources, and toolkits are written by real-world practitioners and thought leaders. They are used globally by audiences of all levels, from students to C-suite executives.

Our high-quality publications cover all IT governance, risk, and compliance frameworks, and are available in a range of formats. This ensures our customers can access the information they need in the way they need it.

Our other publications about cybersecurity include:

- *IT Governance – An international guide to data security and ISO 27001/ISO 27002, Eighth edition* by Alan Calder and Steve Watkins, *www.itgovernancepublishing.co.uk/product/it-governance-an-international-guide-to-data-security-and-iso-27001-iso-27002-eighth-edition*

- *ISO/IEC 27001:2022 – An introduction to information security and the ISMS standard* by Steve Watkins, *www.itgovernancepublishing.co.uk/product/iso-iec-27001-2022*

- *Well-being in the workplace – A guide to resilience for individuals and teams* by Sarah Cook, *www.itgovernancepublishing.co.uk/product/well-being-in-the-workplace*

For more information on ITGP and branded publishing services, and to view our full list of publications, visit *www.itgovernancepublishing.co.uk*.

To receive regular updates from ITGP, including information on new publications in your area(s) of interest, sign up for our newsletter at *www.itgovernancepublishing.co.uk/topic/newsletter*.

Branded publishing

Through our branded publishing service, you can customize ITGP publications with your organization's branding.

Find out more at

www.itgovernancepublishing.co.uk/topic/branded-publishing-services.

Related services

ITGP is part of GRC International Group, which offers a comprehensive range of complementary products and services to help organizations meet their objectives.

For a full range of resources on cybersecurity visit *www.itgovernanceusa.com/shop/category/cybersecurity*.

Training services

The IT Governance training program is built on our extensive practical experience designing and implementing management systems based on ISO standards, best practice, and regulations.

Our courses help attendees develop practical skills and comply with contractual and regulatory requirements. They also support career development via recognized qualifications.

Learn more about our training courses in cybersecurity and view the full course catalog at *www.itgovernanceusa.com/training*.

Professional services and consultancy

We are a leading global consultancy of IT governance, risk management, and compliance solutions. We advise organizations around the world on their most critical issues, and present cost-saving and risk-reducing solutions based on international best practice and frameworks.

We offer a wide range of delivery methods to suit all budgets, timescales, and preferred project approaches.

Find out how our consultancy services can help your organization at *www.itgovernanceusa.com/consulting*.

Industry news

Want to stay up to date with the latest developments and resources in the IT governance and compliance market? Subscribe to our Weekly Round-up newsletter and we will send you mobile-friendly emails with fresh news and features about your preferred areas of interest, as well as unmissable offers and free resources to help you successfully start your projects. *www.itgovernanceusa.com/weekly-round-up*.

EU for product safety is Stephen Evans, The Mill Enterprise Hub, Stagreenan, Drogheda, Co. Louth, A92 CD3D, Ireland. (servicecentre@itgovernance.eu)